You are

Invited

To

To

CHINGLISH

In Pictures and Verse

Mark F. Harris

TAY ATTENT ION
Is self-published by Mark F. Harris

©2008 by Mark F. Harris
All Rights Reserved
Printed in the USA

ISBN 978-0-615-25503-3

Also by Mark F. Harris:
The Harris Solution to Rubik's Cube
A Distant Place
The Missionary Journals of Edward Daniel Harris
Letters from China
Mark's Little Joke Book
Letters from Serbia (With Luree Condie Harris)

For additional copies of this book email
mlharris@pacbell.net

Introduction

Being unfamiliar with Chinese cultural and knowing essentially little of the Mandarin language, we arrived in Beijing in the late summer of 1996. In just a few days my wife, Luree and I were scheduled to begin teaching English to students at a teachers college; students who had studied English for six to eight years in the Chinese public schools. For most of the students, we would be their first native English teachers.

In walking the streets of Beijing we noticed that many businesses displayed signs in English as well as in Chinese. We quickly came to realize that having knowledge of and using English was important to the Chinese people. We were quite impressed. Perhaps English was some universal language. However, we noticed that many of these English signs—even though most were understandable—had misspelled words or displayed rather awkward construction. At first, we found a bit of humor in these signs, but in studying them, we began to ask "why", "how" and "who" questions about their origin.

In becoming acquainted with our students, we learned they had been taught English by some of the nearly half-million native Chinese teachers of English in the public schools of the country. And of course, these teachers were the product of the same school system. Most likely, some of the better students were responsible for creating the business signs in English. We concluded that English as taught in China was not American English, nor British English, but Chinese English, or as we came to learn "Chinglish". This is what we were reading on the signs.

It would take those who are more scholarly to answer the "why", "how" and "who" questions of Chinglish, but as we attempted to learn a bit of the Chinese language—which was not much—we realized that word-for-word translation was not possible. Probably the Chinese who knew English best were not those hired to create signs in English. Perhaps business owners were not really concerned that the English be correct, but displayed it for appearance, their audience being local people rather than foreigners.

In teaching English composition, I became acquainted with Chinese English in reading hundreds of short essays. Even though I made many suggestions on how to improve their writing, I was fascinated with my students' ability to use almost poetic imagery in describing simple daily activities. I concluded that even though they wrote in English, somehow the combined Chinese language, culture and thought pattern was superimposed over the English. I was most impressed with their writing; so impressed that I began making a collection of essays. After returning to the United States, I published a book: <u>A Distant Place</u>, containing the 230 best student essays.

In traveling throughout China, I almost always carried a camera. Consequently, I took thousands of photographs: of people, buildings, flowers, tourist attractions and of course business and tourist signs in Chinglish. Also, from student essays, I copied the ten most unique sentences for each week and in subsequent teaching exercises had the students attempt to rewrite them. By year's end I had a sizable collection of Chinglish sentences.

This book contains many photographs of Chinglish business and tourist signs interspersed with student Chinglish sentences.

TAY ATTENT ION

The photographs have been placed in the order that someone might encounter while visiting China for a few days.

Mark F. Harris
2008

TAY ATTENT ION

History is an old subject in China.

*China, an old country,
has a long history of 5000 years.*

Dedication

This book is respectfully dedicated to all those who have visited China and experienced language and culture as displayed in signs.

TAY ATTENT ION

I was born a baby child.

I will gratitude my father forever.

A Visit to China

Fortunate we were that the pilot of our airliner
chose to land at a

Finding our passports and visas in order
we successfully went through the

After taking such a long flight we were anxious to locate a

TAY ATTENT ION

I'm not sad or worry about it.

I have a family of four numbers.

The next order of business was to find lodging.
We chose to stay at the

Out on the street we looked for a place to have lunch.
We dined at the most

Being anxious to become acquainted with some of the
unique attractions it was important to find the

TAY ATTENT ION

My brother is a very handsome boy.

John's two eyes are very small and most of them are black.

TAY ATTENT ION

We wanted to have a slow-paced view of the country-side.
At our hotel we discovered there were

We decided to visit an

TAY ATTENT ION

He was blind in his eyes.

*When I was young,
I made a lot of spectacles of myself.*

TAY ATTENT ION

And of course there was

When purchasing a ticket
we learned that even

TAY ATTENT ION

*The spectacles is a set
which is worn before one's eyes.*

It really makes me eye-opened.

However, young children received a break in price.

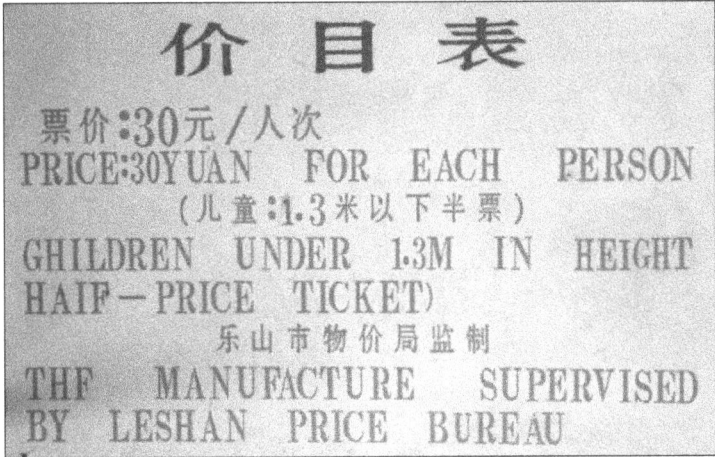

But of course for some there was

They were to use

So, childhood may certainly be fairly happy.

I feel lucky now that I am not so tall.

TAY ATTENT ION

Soon we discovered a long list of rules posted as a

> **NOTICE TO TOURIST**
>
> 1. Please admit to tourist spot after you buy a ticket conscientiously. Once tickets leave the booking office will not be returned.
> 2. Strictly forbid climbing ancient building or carving and drawing anywhere.
> 3. Strictly forbid carrying things which are easy to burn or explode to get into the tourist spot.
> 4. Please don't spit and litter the waste material anywhere.
> 5 Strictly forbid fighting, getting drunk and create a disturbance in the tourist spot.
> 6 Each tourist organization guide must hold the guide card issued by state tourist bureau, then allowed to enter tourist spot to guide.
> 7 Strictly forbid doing any unlawful activities in the tourist spot.
> 8 Each who violate above-mentioned stipulate will be punished with according to the seriousness of his case.

It was comforting to know that the tourist spot was

TAY ATTENT ION

*My story may not compare very well
with my other peers.*

*I haven't got an indefinite idea
about my future.*

TAY ATTENT ION

In the beautiful country-side we paused to

Which was a reminder of being in the

We were also instructed to

*So, my future has been
a question occupying
my mind since my childhood.*

*A dream is the motivity to inspirit
you to stride along.*

TAY ATTENT ION

And to

> 爱护环境 勿扔杂物
> 爱护花木 请勿攀折
> Take care of our surroundings.
> No littering.
> Take care of the flower.
> No picking.

In coming across a shrine or other monument
it was important to

> 保持安静环境
> 庙内严禁用喇叭
> KEEP ENVIRONMENT QUIET
> TRUMPET IS FOR BIDDEN IN TEMPLE

*Maybe one day, I will become the mother
of my own child.*

*Mom saw me out with that gentle smile
as usual on her face which touched
my heart deeply.*

TAY ATTENT ION

As well as to

美化环境
BEAUTIFY THE ENVIRONMENT

保护环境卫生
PROTECT ENVIRONMENTAL SANITATION

And to

请自觉遵守公共秩序。
CONSCIENTIONSLY OBSERVE PUBLIC ORDER PLEASE

请注意讲究卫生,不乱扔杂物
KEEP CLEAN PLEASE DON'T THROW SUNDRY RANDOMLG

请勿吸烟,注意防火,保护泰山。
NO SMOKING PLEASE FIRE PREVENTION ATTENTION PROTECT MOUNT TAI

And above all, there should be

请勿随地吐痰
请勿乱抛果皮纸屑
禁止吸烟
NO SPITTING LITTER SMOKING

TAY ATTENT ION

*She smiled with
tears in her eyes by the door.*

*There was a knob in the middle
of one edge of the door, which was gone.*

TAY ATTENT ION

After our excursion into the country-side we returned to the city for lunch and found the

However, there was much confusion when being told

So we immediately walked across the street to the

TAY ATTENT ION

*It was a heavy snowy day when
I was seven years old.*

*I was wrapped up pretty well
to keep the cold out by mother,
leaving only two eyes.*

Following a delicious meal we paid our bill at the

In planning to go shopping for the remainder of the day we immediately noticed an

TAY ATTENT ION

*Whether it is because
my own fault or not,
I have many obstacles in
my path of proceeding.*

*I was stumbled by a stone
and fell to the ground.*

Being hot and thirsty, our next stop was at the

Another store of interest was the

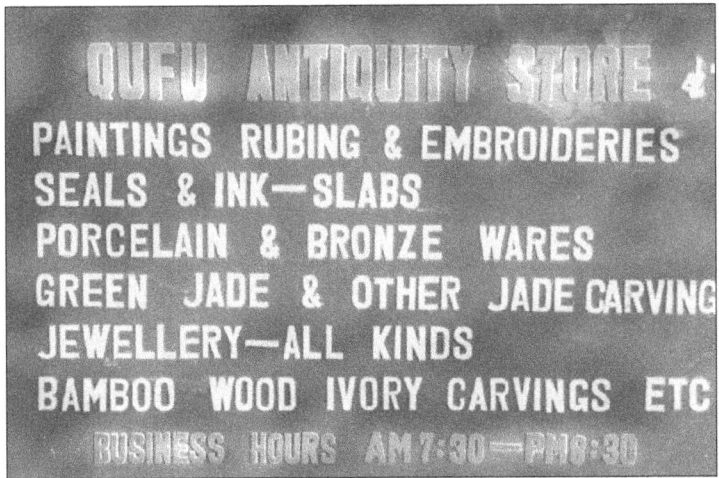

TAY ATTENT ION

*She lay on the ground,
hair disheveled, eyes closed,
arms and legs stretched out
without any vigor.*

*Tears ran down my rosy cheeks
and into the mouth and it's salty.*

As we continued to walk the streets, driving by was the

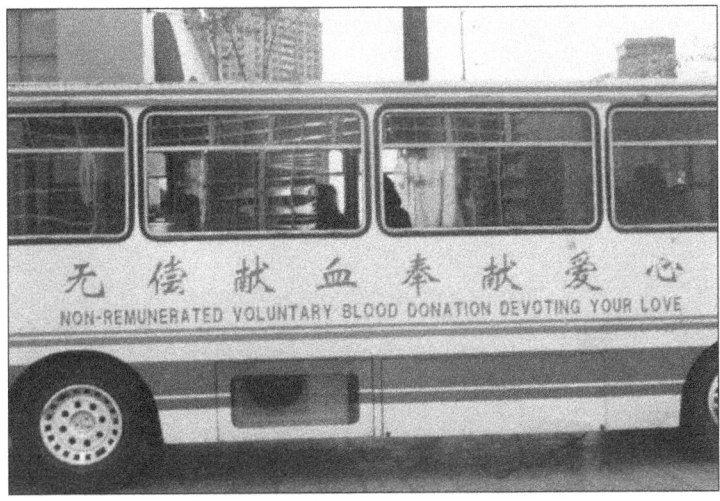

bus.

Having taken a large number of photographs we needed to find a place to

TAY ATTENT ION

*My brain was so blank
that it couldn't control my body.*

*I was so embarrassed,
I wished there was a hole in the earth
that would swallow me down.*

TAY ATTENT ION

Realizing our camera had a problem
required finding a place for

Nearby was a shop that promised to

REPAIR CAMERA FASTLY

Also a shop that we might need later was the

NEWCHINA PROFESSIONAL HAIRESSING CENTRE

TAY ATTENT ION

*And tears overflew my lids
and run down along my cheeks.*

*While standing in the field,
looking upward, you see the stars,
and you think they are
at certain heights,
which seem reachable
by jumping.*

It was reassuring to know that for better sight
we could visit

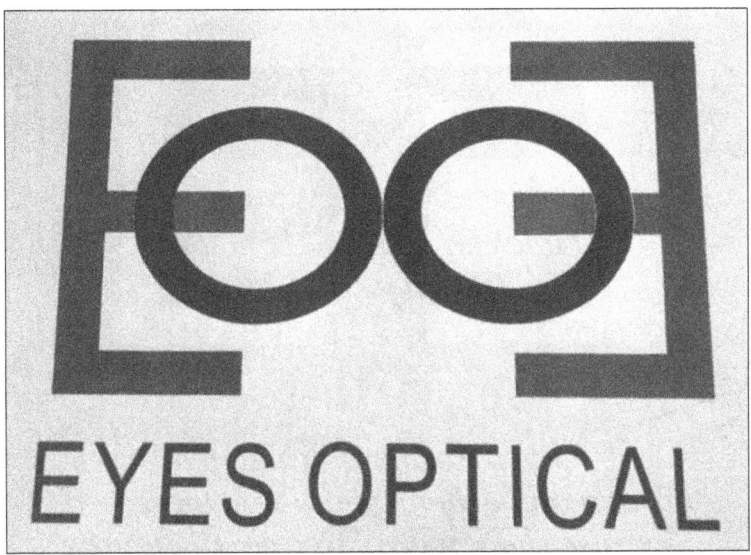

Or the

TAY ATTENT ION

*Time can be traced back to
fifteen years ago.*

*When Father got married,
burden on Father's shoulders increased,
because there were three small mouths
crying for feeding.*

TAY ATTENT ION

Any tourists driving may find a need to visit the

If anyone became ill treatment could be through

We walked by the

TAY ATTENT ION

*When grandpa told me what
and how he studied at that time,
I saw his eyes were twinkled.*

*It was there that he met a
pretty girl and several years later,
she became my grandmother.*

For money exchange there was

For communication we could use

Or perhaps obtain a cell phone through

TAY ATTENT ION

*My mother has six children
and she is in the middle.*

*She was a graceful and
well-behaviored girl.*

*I loved her deeply;
so did she.*

Relief from boredom in China might come by visiting

Or by viewing the

WAXWORKS EXHIBITIONS OF CHINESE FAMOUS FIGURES TICKET OFFICE

When pressures seemed overwhelming there were

CONTRACT-STRESSING AND PROMISE-KEEPING ENTERPRISES
QINGDAO BUSINESS EXECUTIVE MANAGEMENT BUREAU

TAY ATTENT ION

*They have done so much to us children,
I will do the same to them.*

*No matter,
whether you know it or not,
you should offer your sincerity and love.*

TAY ATTENT ION

Heading for our hotel we were fortunate to find some

And then for dinner we stopped at

For evening entertainment we could attend

TAY ATTENT ION

*The first glimpse of his white hairs
on the temples, and then
the lines of years.*

"Papa is old and tired," murmured I.

However, he is younger than his age.

Or slip into the

But we chose to go to

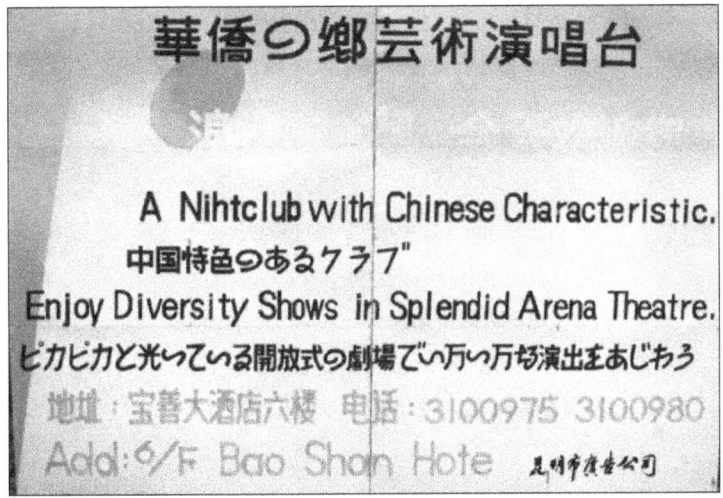

Back at our hotel we noticed the fire extinguishers on each floor were filled with

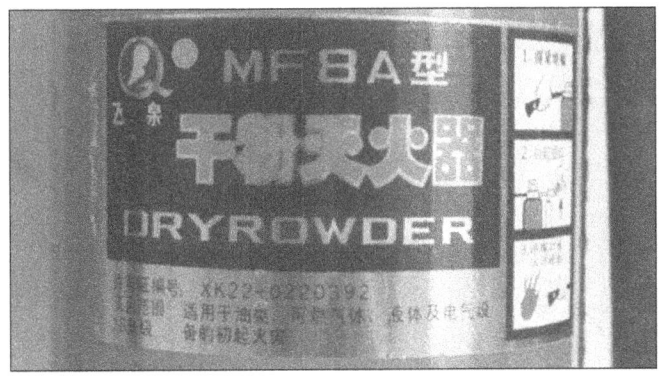

*He was laid off when I passed
the college entrance examination
because of age.*

*After the entrance
examination to college,
the destiny settled me to
the teacher's college
out of my expectation.*

On the second day as tourists in China we wanted to visit historical and cultural places. For convenience, we each bought a

Along the way was the shop of an

TAY ATTENT ION

*As a freshman,
I was almost curious
about everything.*

*I am eager to learn what I don't know.
In every exam I almost got
the worst mark.*

TAY ATTENT ION

An attraction that caught our attention was the

Others were the

My university life looks like dull.

*After entering college,
I eagered to have a part-time job.*

*I have a smattery knowledge
about painting.*

And the

The main goal for the day was to find our

TAY ATTENT ION

*The panda
is considered by scientists
to be one of the oldest animals
that lived through a long time.*

*I hope one day in the near future,
I will sit down and take up writing
as my life-through career.*

TAY ATTENT ION

Fortunately our schedule fit with the

*I have learned these good
characteristics from my beloved
foreign teacher, Mr. Harris
and his best half,
Mrs. Harris.*

*We will remember you and your wife
at the bottom of our hearts.*

TAY ATTENT ION

It was necessary to find

But we weren't alone when arriving at the

*I still have a long way to go
in the future.*

*I am not qualified to be a good teacher,
because I know little about society,
which is a shortcoming
for a teacher.*

To get to the right place we needed to take the

For the ride we were advised to
hang on tight and

TAY ATTENT ION

*Where there's a will there's a way,
isn't it?*

*I had a fight with my friend
over trivials.*

*Anxiety was in company
with me those days.*

TAY ATTENT ION

Foreigners needing assistance might find helpful services offered at the

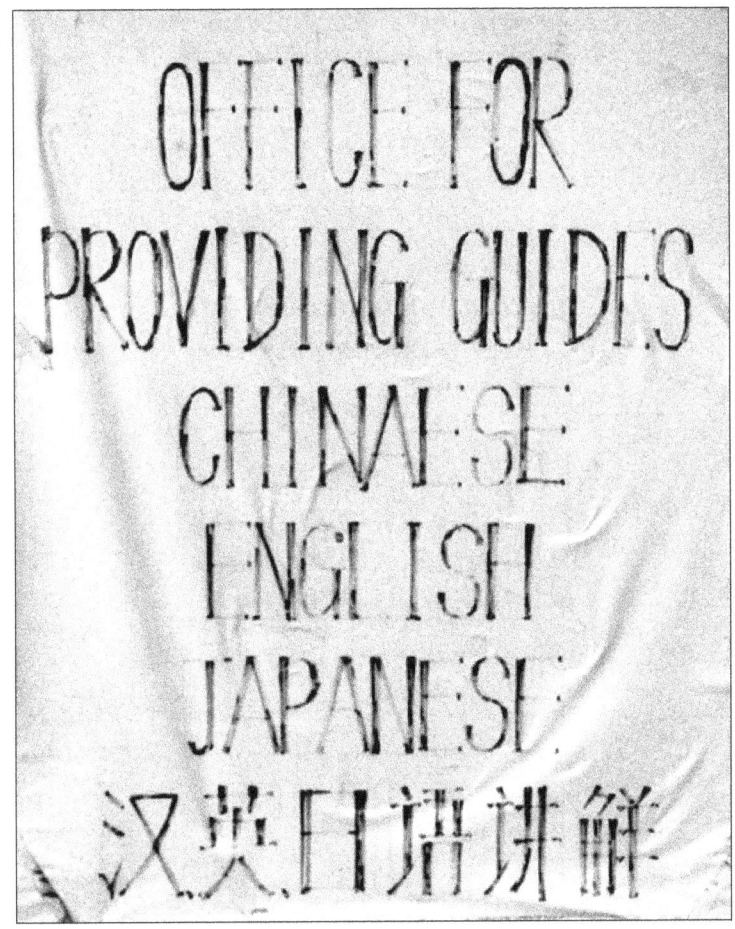

TAY ATTENT ION

*I didn't stop eating apples
until my stomach couldn't
stand one any more.*

*After eating them
my heart seesawed between
delight and upset.*

TAY ATTENT ION

Once in the facility we noticed many commercial enterprises and were anxious to enter the

Here was the offer to purchase a

TAY ATTENT ION

*The
sour bitterness
and deep love
was two streams
flowing in my heart.*

*My face is ugly,
but I don't feel sorry for it.*

There was fierce competition between sellers.
Some one could have a

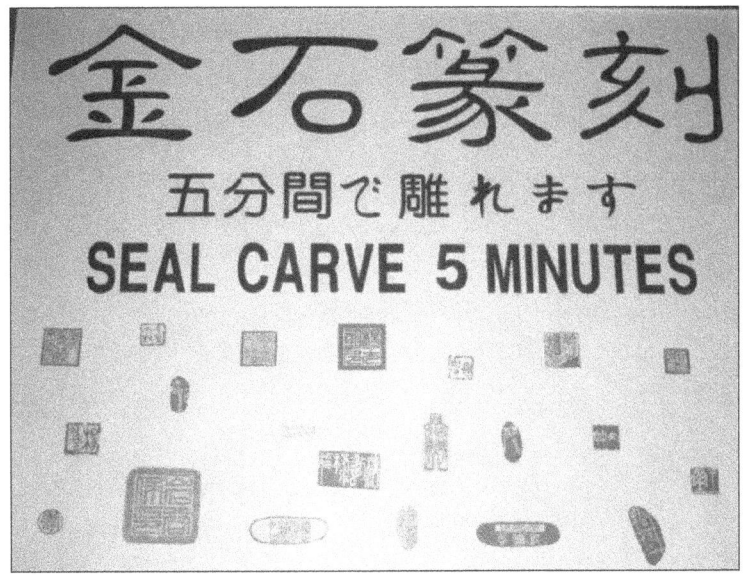

Or just walk across the street and observe
some one

TAY ATTENT ION

*I flew into angry
and climbed on a stone wall.*

*Its yellow background
is dotted with green and brown flowers
here and there.*

TAY ATTENT ION

For refreshment consider sipping some

TAY ATTENT ION

*By God's help,
we would succeed in stealing
a bag of big apples each.*

*If I was clever enough,
I would rather steal apples or pears
instead of peaches.*

*After supper,
we climbed over the wall
to go home that abuts my
grandmother's house.*

Or, perhaps it would be a

TAY ATTENT ION

*Parting time
seems to put another
coat of shadow
on our minds.*

*At last,
my nature of stubbornness
got the upper hand over me.*

There might be confusion about the direction,
but one necessary stop would be to visit the

And for the high point of the visit
it may be exciting to just

TAY ATTENT ION

*On the way home,
our bicycle was stumbled over a stone
and it bumped suddenly.*

*I didn't know
what kind of destination
I was heading to.*

Perhaps overlooked was the possibility to have some one

Being late in the day it was time to

TAY ATTENT ION

*I stood in shallow water,
watching my friends
play with admire.*

*The water was flowing
through my toes.*

*When the water flowed
down my head,
I was gooseflesh
all over.*

In the future an interesting part of China to visit would be

Or

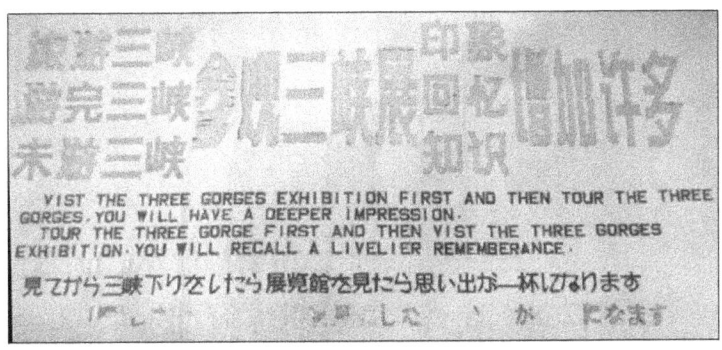

TAY ATTENT ION

One of my dreams is going to Tibet.

*One day in the future
of ten years from now
I will be in Europe
or America.*

TAY ATTENT ION

Overall, we can describe our visit to China as

And of course, the standing invitation is to

As a finale to our tour of China, we can say hurrah, hurrah and

*Try to be a travel agent,
work hard and grasp at
the opportunity.*

*I won't be able to trust sales people
nor my roommates.*

*In the end, I attribute myself
to a contradictory person.*

And

Did you know that

PAY ATTENTION

*When I don't agree with others,
I'd like to keep my opinions
rather than argue with them.*

*In order to release their intension,
they need a good and patient listener.*

TAY ATTENT ION

In reading this little book of Chinglish you have been very good to

From one

To another,

Thank you.

*Last, you may meet your
Mr. Right or Mrs. Right in your college,
who will become your future
husband or future wife.*

*Then I counted my fingers
to wait for his letters.*

www.ingramcontent.com/pod-product-compliance
Lightning Source LLC
Chambersburg PA
CBHW031416040426
42444CB00005B/601